More Praise for *Secret Histories*

Secret Histories, by Michael McInnis, is a journey from sea to sky, where you "see the stars in each swell, as if land exists only at the pleasure of the ocean." Mermaids walk amongst us, and fortune may allow us to trace their tattoos with our tongues. There are secret messages in storms and unquenchable thirsts, and a girl named Lucy, whose skin we can't stop thinking about. McInnis shows us "how we dream up gods in our desert consciousness," knowing that all the while, the sharks feed below.
—Heather Sullivan, author of *Method Acting for the Afterlife*

Secret Histories

Michael McInnis

Hannah,
There are many
paths to poetry.

2020

Červená Barva Press
Somerville, Massachusetts

Červená Barva Press
P.O. Box 440357
W. Somerville, MA 02144-3222

www.cervenabarvapress.com

Bookstore: www.thelostbookshelf.com

Cover Photo from the collection of Lauren Leja

Cover Design: Michael McInnis

ISBN: 978-1-950063-10-9

Library of Congress Control Number: 2019946711

Distributed by Small Press Distribution: www.spdbooks.org

Acknowledgments

Anti-Heroin Chic · Medals

The Bees Are Dead · Something about Talking Animals

Chiron Review · Old man lived two doors down died

Commonline Journal · British Soldiers

Corner Club Press · Secret Lives of the Famous

Deadly Writers Patrol · Travelogue of Diego Garcia; Thank You for Your Service

Five on the Fifth published a different version of Swimming

In Between Hangovers · A Secret History of the Solar System; Empty Headed

Literary Yard · The Weathermen

Live Nude Poems · A Secret History of Existentialism

Lummox · An Ostrich Feather and Three Gold Watch Fobs

Naugatuck River Review · Storm Coming Up the Bay

Nixes Mate Review · At the Fisherman's Feast of the Madonna Del Soccorso di Sciacca; Hagiography of Magellan

One Sentence Poems · 4 Lines, 33 Words; Silence Between the Leaves; Travelogue of Australia

OxMag · Letters to Travel Agencies

Right Hand Mini · Canadian Tanker Down Chelsea Creek

Muddy River Review · This is what you say to a person who is dying

Unknown Journal · Astronauts

Unlikely Stories · 7 sentences Hogan's Bar & Grill

White Knuckle Press published slightly different versions of several pieces as a digital chapbook, *Secret Histories*

Yellow Chair Review published a slightly different version of Lucy the Magdalene Requiem

Contents

Let me tell you about the sea.   3
Bioluminescence   4
Canadian Tanker Down Chelsea Creek   3
British Soldiers   4
Travelogue of Australia   5
Travelogue of Diego Garcia   6
Travelogue of Hong Kong   7
Travelogue of Korea   8
Travelogue of Nagasaki   9
Travelogue of the South Pacific   10
Lucy the Magdalene   11
Viva la revolucion!   14
Can You Hear Me Now   15
4 lines, 33 words   16
Fantail   17
Astronauts   18
Life Out of Balance   19
Empty Headed   20
On Tracking Comets   21
On Tracking Moons   22
Boiling   23
Cheating   24
Cutting   26
Crackling   27
Dancing   29
Eating   30
Minding   32

Plunging   33
Swimming   35
Tattooing   36
Seven Sentences Set in Hogan's Bar & Grill   37
The Beatles Agnostics   40
Scenes from a Commute   42
Hagiography of Kafka   43
Hagiography of Magellan   44
Ötzi   45
Urban Renewal   46
Letters to Travel Agencies   47
An Ostrich Feather and Three Gold Watch Fobs   49
Something About Talking Animals   50
Postcards from a Parallel Universe   51
Stratospheric Microwaves Are No Cure for Acne   53
Secret Messages   54
A Secret History of Acadia   55
A Secret History of Existentialism   57
A Secret History of Exorcism   58
A Secret History of Kahoutek   59
A Secret History of the Solar System   60
A Secret History of Woodworking   61
Secret Moments in the Lives of the Famous   62
Alien Spacecraft   66
An Alien Encounter   68
Broken Window   69
Wicked Gravity   71
Memory Illuminated   73
At the Fisherman's Feast of the
    Madonna Del Soccorso di Sciacca   74

The Tourists   75
The Weathermen   76
Storm Coming Up The Bay   78
Thirst   80
My Old Captain Died Yesterday   81
The old man lived two doors down died.   82
Reincarnation   84
Lucy the Magdalene Requiem   85
Medals   87
Thank You for Your Service   88
This is what you say to a person who is dying   99
Silence between the leaves   103

"Don't be afraid to face the facts, and never lose your ability to ask the questions: Why? and How?"
— Immanuel Velikovsky

Secret Histories

Let me tell you about the sea.

Let me tell you about the sea.
The way the sky mutinies and
the stars leave shimmering
kisses on a tattooed back.
Each ship lost in tropical doldrums,
adrift, dead in the water,
where cyclones form
and once cannibals feasted.

While working aloft,
under a white-knuckled sun,
I dreamt of inked daughters.
Is this how Fletcher Christian felt?
Melville?
Is this the way to a bread fruit paradise?

Let me tell you about the sea.
The way it mutinies against the sky,
swallows the stars
and washes away an aphotic night.

Bioluminescence

The coal of a cigarette
cupped in mid-air
on the port bridge wing
appeared as just another
star while the ship wedged
through the ocean
leaving a frothy glowing
wake of bioluminescence.
The frigate become a
moonless target
on a dusty sea,
lost in a decaying orbit
as if a tin can in space
like a tin can at sea
had slipped over the edge.

Canadian Tanker Down Chelsea Creek

We watched a Canadian tanker pushed backwards, down
Chelsea Creek, by a trio of tugboats.

On the tanker's fo'c'sle lay three boxes of moldy tissues,
a rusty license plate, a one-pound box of six-penny nails
and, we later discovered, an address book with only one
address repeated on each page.

The Flat Earth Society leaving counter-revolutionary
clues, you said, staking their claim, knowing the tides
would protest.

Something to do with tectonics and phrenology,
I said.

Isn't tectonics phrenology writ planet wide,
you said.

Yes, the mountains on that plate precipitates criminality,
I said. The occipital rivers and valleys on another plate
indicates imbecility. But what about our claim?

I gambled that away, you said. The tides won. The house
always wins.

We watched the tanker whisper into the fog, riding high,
heading back north where wild horses run, where the
glaciers stopped at the edge of the continent, eroded by
fifty foot tides.

British Soldiers

He listed one of the Charles as an emergency contact –

Simic
Fort
Darwin

– on the form the nurse handed him reeling from
ingesting red helmeted British soldiers.

Sheet lightening still crackling across his eyes as if Orion
had risen during the summer, winter only a name given to
war heroes who walked in heavy gales through a pocked
landscape.

The tree down across the cratered path, *Cladonia cristatella*
and *Trebouxia erici* holding out for new growth, luminous
from the night's rain, bitter and musty tasting still as they
pumped his stomach of the lichen.

Travelogue of Australia

From Circular Quay to King's Cross, sailors traffic in lies
and tattoo the sky with debauchery.

Travelogue of Diego Garcia

1

The Indian Ocean off Diego Garcia swallowed a ship-
mate. The coral glowed pink and yellow and came
rushing up at him as he thrashed to reach the surface. So,
this is it then. No more midwatches on a ship at sea. No
more evenings back home, the smell of butane and beef
raked through the air. Sharks told the sailor their secrets
as the sea spread summer clouds of blood.

2

We got high and bet on coconut crabs sprinting across
crushed coral roads. There was time enough for sonar
and ships and sharks. I heard, someone said, that Great
Whites won't bite you when you're drunk.

Travelogue of Hong Kong

From the top of Victoria Peak the city looked scrubbed
clean, while drunk and freshly tattooed sailors, off a fast
frigate anchored in the middle of the harbor, lurched
through the streets of the Wan-Chai where topless barmaids
wear shawls because it's always winter inside the pubs.

Travelogue of Korea

I felt helpless in the kimchee tinted smog, hungover on
an ecological scale, reeling from spending the night with a
girl in a room heated by a small coal brazier, her skin pure
and blemish free, her black hair hooding and caressing
my face when she hovered over me, smiling and laughing.
All I could see was the ocean in her eyes.

Travelogue of Nagasaki

On my ship, you could neither confirm nor deny the presence of nuclear weapons. In the Nagasaki of my memory, in the Nagasaki of my dreams, the plot varies little. Sounds of children playing and birds singing drift through a park. A bicyclist, delivering newspapers, rides over the Megane Bridge. A group of young women walk to Mass at the Urakami Cathedral. An elderly man, yoked with arthritis, leans against a building and looks at his watch. A trolley passes. After the earth is scorched and the sky tastes like metal and smells of burnt flesh, a tear in the atmosphere mends, leaving a jagged scar and a polished black monolith that reflects the shadows of the lucky ones.

Travelogue of the South Pacific

On an island yet to be discovered – navigational maps
referenced only deep sea volcanoes – where crystal pools
of sweet blue liquid nourished the flora and fauna, where
the cognoscenti tended interior vineyards and the hoo-
ligans, pedestrians and sailors argued essential questions
of the universe, fears of alien encounters remained un-
known, or so it was rumored, except among shipwreck
survivors who were quarantined to the side of the island
where seals and reptiles lounged and where sharks swam
the hypersaline lagoon.

Lucy the Magdalene

You're cute, she said, I'm Lucy.

I told her she was beautiful. I followed her off the base over the Olongapo River where boys dove in to dig coins out of the muck thrown by sailors who laughed every time a boy came up covered in shit.

Exchanged dollars for pesos at a shack that gave packs of gum instead of coin change and jumped on a trike to Lucy's house. The street grid laid out like a game of Mikado. The deeper we drove into the city, the more I realized that if I had to, I'd never find my way out. I was totally dependent upon Lucy.

Over Lucy's bed hung a wooden crucifix that she later told me her mother had sent her. The eyes of Christ were hollow, its emaciated body dripped with blood.

Lucy bent down, sucked my nipples and then lunged at my neck. I wanted to scream and looked up at the blood-soaked Christ and thought Lucy might be a vampire. Now, you won't butterfly, she said when she had finished leaving a necklace of purple bruises.

The next day I did not have duty. Lucy suggested we go out to the provinces to swim at the beach. I have to get my swimsuit, I said.

It alright. We don't need one.

_____

A green haze rose out of the jungle and settled on the bay. In the light, Lucy's skin looked like the color of creamy peanut butter. She stood in the surf, naked, splashing herself and laughing while I dropped my shorts and pulled off my sneakers. The single bottle of San Miguel we purchased from a street vendor, spilled into the sand. But Lucy only laughed louder. She turned and dove into the frothy brown waves and disappeared under the water. A golden Venus returning to the sea.

Lucy surfaced twenty feet out. I ran down to the surf, splashed and waved my arms. Lucy swam away from me, squealing and laughing. I could see she loved being naked in the sea. She loved being naked on land too.

She didn't care if anyone saw her. Later, she told me that she wished the nuns on Cebo Island, where she was born, could see her naked on the beach. She wished a priest would walk by. The girls from Luzon were always telling her to act less crazy. Americans won't marry crazy Filipino girls. Lucy told me she was not sure if she wanted to marry an American sailor. She loved being free, drinking San Miguel in the morning, swimming in the ocean naked and fucking on the beach. I could not argue with her. At nineteen, that's all I wanted to do.

Out in the bay, I could still smell the jungle, the heavy fecund earth that was the color of Lucy's skin. I loved Lucy's skin. All the previous night I had drawn my fingers over its blemish free perfection. Sometimes, I thought I could smell the Philippines, and the ocean, the jungle and the hot blanket of stars in her skin.

———

I swam like a shark and came in under Lucy and scooped her into my arms lifting her up out of the water. She laughed, screamed and kissed my face. In the water, her skin felt like paradise.

Let's live on the beach forever, I said.

Oh you silly, we can't stay here. Your ship will leave and you'll get in trouble.

I don't care. I want to live on this beach with you. I want to swim naked with you. I want to fuck you on the sand every night.

You are very silly, Lucy said and swam back to shore.

After we fucked on the sand and lay sunning, half asleep, thirsty because the San Miguel had spilled, Lucy turned to me and ran her fingers up and down my skinny chest. When you leave will you send me postage stamps from your ship?

Why?

So I can write you, silly. And before you leave, will you give me twenty-five extra dollars so I can buy new shoes and some food?

Okay, I will. But why talk like that? My ship isn't leaving for another week.

I was just thinking, Lucy said and kissed me.

On the way to catch a Jeepney back to Magsaysay Blvd, in the jungle, we heard a family celebration. Some of the men carried a dog, its throat already cut, up from the stream and threw it on the fire where the fur hissed and scudded. Lucy tried to pull me away to tell me her secrets of the Philippines. But I drank a San Miguel I had bought from the family and watched a guy scrape the dog's fur off with the edge of a machete.

Viva la revolucion!

I fell for her revolutionary spiel, our kisses in the back-seat of her cab, the way she licked my nipples, how she felt through her yoga pants. In my 'cuntry', she said, the disappeared populate the mountains and pampas, the seas and rivers. She gave me a copy of Galeano's *Memory of Fire* trilogy. I followed her to South America and fought the junta with her. We fucked after every raid on government installations, filthy and desperate, as if every night was a full moon and we were wolves. The last time I saw her she commandeered a narrow-gauge locomotive with a famous punk rock singer and headed west to the hills to root out fascists and translate Russell Edson and Charles Simic in to Esperanto, leaving me to clean up the carnage and run the damned country until, eventually, the military overthrew the government and dragged me behind a tank through the streets of the capital.

Can You Hear Me Now

We rocketed our children to the future and watched them land on planets with flinty cellular coverage, free of us and our gravity.

4 lines, 33 words
(after John Cage)

More than halfway through I'm beginning to think
we met in a silence so deafening that
the only sound you hear is your heart beating
as if tinnitus has become a new religion.

Fantail

We stood on the fantail, you and I, come off a watch
exhausted and awake, watching each arm of a turbulent V
rake clouds across the horizon just out of reach from the
frigate, while beneath each swell, beneath the savagery and
treachery of a ceaseless sea, glided creatures and whales
and the devilish beauty that is a shark.

I said: *I see the stars in each swell, as if land exists only at the
pleasure of the ocean.*

You said: *I see constellations from my rack three decks down. I
see jaundice and bloody tattoos. I smell hops and barley, puke
and piss in every port. I taste the burn of crystal meth down the
back of my throat on every midwatch. I see naked islanders and
Marxists rebels and the sheet lightning of a migraine. I feel the
hot blaze of an atomic bomb and take a sighting on a hole in
the sky. I see sonar contacts and battle groups. I see helicopters
burning and the desert aflame. I see my burial at sea, flag draped,
wrapped like a mummy and weighted down with iron and steel.*

Destiny had always discounted her neighbor's complaints of flashing lights, multi-colored streamers and shrill noises to failed weather balloon experiments, rocket circuitry malfunctions and distracted sonarmen until she woke one morning to find a team of three astronauts in her backyard. One astronaut sat against the far fence, his head slumped on his chest weighed down by the white helmet, shimmering like a dwarf sun and enveloping Destiny's backyard in a vaporous whiteness. The other two astronauts lay on the ground. Clouds like sprinkled white asterisks reflected on the darkened visors of their helmets.

Life Out of Balance

A man came home from work and found liquid from
Jupiter seeping under his front door. All the automats
broke down from an increase in sunspot activity, but the
Earth's albedo ratio remained stable. The man felt a sense
of longing for a dry city, a desert city with banners furled
in the wind, a city strafed with colors and populated
with hawkers selling moisture, a city where the men and
women are clad only in tattoos, a city where music is the
lingua franca. We remained silent and watched the man
vacuum up the liquid while listening to a contra-bassoon
soloist play the main theme to *Koyaanisqatsi*.

Empty Headed

It's easy being a Monday morning Trepannist. What's a little 3rd-eye pain, blood down your face, oxygen flooding your skull, electric drill hanging above your head. Light shatters the walls of the room as if a parallel universe exists just the other side of the door and everything you touch becomes anti-matter. This is how we dream up gods in our desert consciousness, she said, pulling the drill closer.

On Tracking Comets

The weather was mild and sprinkling. An angry comet, mad that it was nothing more than a dirty ice ball and vowing to do real damage someday if only it wasn't stuck in this orbit, scorched across the solar system. There seemed no point waiting for the comet's return.

On Tracking Moons

We stood watching a new moon circling Jupiter. A
screaming moon, full of gadgetry and gimcrackery.
That moon, that screaming moon catapulted us over
handlebars where we landed on the windshield of a
passing murmuring moon. We left a perfect imprint of
our body on the passing murmuring moon, sliding and
tumbling in orbit past still more moons.

Boiling

Poplar met him in a photography workshop at an artist's retreat. In the darkroom, his tattoos glowed. At first, they scared her, like seeing fire under water, seething boiling black ink in the red light. But the eagles on the back of his neck, like yin and yang totems, she wanted to devour, to lick their secret animal spirits, to find out what protected him. She saved the eagles for last. First, she swallowed the shark's teeth tattooed around his neck.

In high school, he dated the girl who tattooed three lines on her left forearm with a threaded needle and ink. He drove her and her friends around even though his car had lost its power steering and three point turns felt like rounding the Horn.

She and her friends talked about their periods and masturbating in the shower and told him to pretend he was a girl and knew all about vaginas and cramps, but to shut up. So he listened and learned and understood this was a world he could only visit.

He navigated another three-point turn.

They all felt sorry for him, for his struggle, so the girl with the three tattooed lines grabbed his crotch. He's got a boner, she said. They all laughed.

But he still had to navigate the three point turns while they talked and laughed about other boys. How this one kissed like he would kiss his grandmother. And that one left her face slobbered over. How another would wash his hands after he fingered her.

•

He cheated on the girl with the tattooed lines. He didn't understand why. He liked the girl with the three tattooed lines. He liked all her friends. But it was the girl with sepia-colored hair that looked at him in a way the other girls did not.

One day, after class, he saw the girl with the sepia-colored hair walking alone. I want to show you something, she said. She unzipped her shorts. He was surprised she wore no underwear.

•

When the engine seized and he had the car towed to the scrap yard, he stopped seeing the girl with the three tattooed lines and her friends. Without a car, he was back to being a boy. They said hi in the hall but the girl with the sepia-colored hair only smiled and kept walking.

Galen says she's always waiting for a new beginning, a new somewhere that isn't here. He can see it in her eyes, the way the tears always stay behind those imperfectly brown irises and never come out. He tastes her and knows he has a choice. He can help her or help himself. He can't help them both. He doesn't want to compete in the who's crazier game.

·

Galen says she's leaving in the morning to drive across country. She says she's never fucked in the shower. When she comes, her mouth taste like a glacier. The whole bathroom feels rubbery and tastes soapy and she smells like the cleanest person in the world.

·

Galen says she used to cut herself. He says the first time he got hit by a car he wasn't sure if he didn't will it to happen. That he might have avoided all that pain, but didn't want to. Like with my tattoos I don't want to avoid the pain, he says. It's like cutting myself because I want to feel something.

Galen understands this when she's licking his tattoos and tasting the pain that still surfaces.

Crackling

He published Tara's stories in a mis-stapled zine and booked her husband's band to play at a benefit. Tara had a scar between her breasts from when a boy pushed her to the ground and burned cigarettes on her before her mother ever told her what boys were about. She was eleven when her mother died and her father was too afraid to tell her and her sister what boys were about. So, she found out on her own.

●

They met for dinner down in Chinatown. Tara kept wiping lipstick off her tea cup. He liked the way her finger lingered over the russet smudge. He wanted to taste the tea cup and her finger and her mouth. They made out on a bench by the harbor, but it was foggy and cold. She suggested they go to the office where she worked as a receptionist. She had a key and said there was a couch in the employee lounge.

●

They faded after each caress like mis-spent meteorites, flashing across the sky in the rubbery embrace of gravity. They touched moons and tasted stars, seas, salts, sex. They crackled with light, with love and desire, with mania and depression, with dread at the edge of the universe.

•

Every time he saw Tara she grabbed him, kissed him and
told him to eat her. But she only did this when she was
out with her husband and he with his wife. Once, after
a poetry reading, her husband found them kissing. She
wiped lipstick off his cheek and said something about
similes and metaphors while her husband picked at the
desiccated brie set out on a folding table.

Dancing

At his 30th birthday party, Dale found her husband in the bathroom with a poet. The poet zipped up her slacks and he insisted it was not what she thinks. The poet only wanted to show me her new bikini wax, he said.

Dale stood in the middle of the party and shamed the poet, the slut, the skank. After the poet left, followed by five of their mutual friends, Dale got drunk while her husband sat on the sofa watching her dance as she pushed her skirt down exposing the rubble of her belly from the C-section.

Look, she said, see *my* new bikini wax.

They first met at a Vietnamese restaurant. He likes to
think he wasn't drawn to June because of the way she
held and ate a fresh spring roll, dipping it into the peanut
sauce, swirling the roll around the red eye of hot sauce.
He told himself it was her dirty blonde dreadlocks, the
tattoo of an ouroboros behind her left ear, her hazel eyes
and her lips.

When June noticed him looking at her, at first she felt
embarrassed, but that pissed her off. She dipped her finger
in the peanut sauce and spread it over her lips, letting it
drip down her chin. Here, she said, does that complete the
picture, asshole.

•

He was already at the Vietnamese restaurant having a pho
when June walked up to his table. She liked the three
fishing swivels in his left ear and the smudgy black
rectangle tattooed on his left hand. He may be an asshole,
staring at her eating a fresh spring roll, but he looked
interesting with blue eyes, a snarling hairpin scar in the
middle of the cupid's bow of his upper lip, and unwashed,
uncombed hair. Leave your soup, pay the man and come
with me, she said.

•

At her apartment, June kissed his forehead, his eyes, his
mouth, tongued the fishing swivels in his ear. When he

traced the letters of the tattoo between her hip bones with
his tongue:

I-a-m-n-o-t-a-f-r-a-i-d-o-f-s-t-o-r-m-s,

she felt as if he had taken all her air.

Minding

You need a goal in life, Mercedes said. Imagine a
mountain, its base reaching deep in the earth. The ocean
is a cryptic wonder, she said. Your eyes are bluer when you
stand in the light.

In your mind, touch that soft spot below my neck,
between my collar bone, Mercedes said. Now the furrow
behind my ear lobe. Next touch the web between my index
finger and thumb and feel the piece of glass still embedded
beneath my skin from when I fell as a young girl.

Plunging

Velikovsky believes, Page said between sips of coffee, that Venus, once captured in orbit by the Sun, wreaked havoc upon the Earth, plunging us into darkness and terror.

They were in a small cafe somewhere in Montmartre chasing ghosts and the bleeding edge of art, science and desire.

Venus parted seas, rained a nourishing nectar upon the earth and made the sun rise in the east and set in the west where once the opposite was true, she said.

They walked up to Square Louis Michel, holding hands. Paris' birth, like Venus' was written in bloodshed that continues today, Page said.

He did not want to believe it. Could not. Even as bombs went off and his synapses became like controlled avalanches.

•

He raked his fingers across her stomach and left history behind for the rubbery folds of her labia.

We are. Being. Lied to, she said, a flush creeping up from her chest to her neck.

He wanted to rewrite the laws of gravity, to explore quantum mechanics, to catalog the chaotic history of the Higgs Bosun Archipelago, but she wanted only to create her own truth, a long Darwinian slide back to the sea, to yonic perfection.

Do historians know the lies they write, she said. You're no better than a medieval hagiographer of saint's lives. Velikovsky knew the truth about Venus. Velikovsky knew the historian, like the journalist that files phony bylines, was better at exploring the back of his own hand than the thoughts and feelings of people one hundred, two hundred or a thousand years before. Herodotus, Flavius Josephus, Joe Gould, Wells' ridiculous *Outline of History* or Van Loon and his unintentional attempts at humor, everything they know is wrong.

When he pressed her for the truth, she smiled and kissed him.

•

On the last day he saw Page, he was writing a history, an Oort cloud of facts and figures, quotations and anecdotes held together by gluey bits of gravity, plagiarizing false forensics like a party boss buying votes. The sun leeched blood across the earth and Venus promised a new day. How that star came to shine in our sky was a secret history that none dare reveal. She knew its truth, but she only hinted at it and whispered that Newton was a charlatan.

———

Swimming

Ella told him she liked swimming with him.

Those fat old Russians, she said, they're all over the lane and always rubbing up against me.

They do the same to me, he said.

The Russian men in the pool are not headhunters, but the Chinese men share mysteries with the other swimmers as if they are all diving for copies of Mao's *Little Red Book*.

•

The *Hànzi* characters inked on Ella's side told him less about her than the way she swam, training for an open water competition. She high-fived him after he swam a lap of butterfly and thanked him for his military service. He didn't want to be thanked. He wanted a kiss, a grilled cheese sandwich, a glass of iced tea with no lemon or sugar. He wanted to touch her the way the ocean touched her.

•

Ella does not believe in divine retribution, paranormal activity or seismic disturbances. She wants to hear the coda clicks of a sperm whale. At night, in the city, she searches the sky for the shoulder of Orion, but only sees his belt. The Seven Sisters remains an erased smudge of white chalk. If Ella dove with them, the whales could see the stars in her eyes.

Ava set out to fill a vacuum in her life with ink. She
found books and magazines with photographs of tattoos.
There were red and raw devil faces surrounding shaved
vulvas, noses the length of flaccid penises, portraits of
dead rock stars on forearms, great weeping Christ effigies
on backs, petroglyphs dancing like a crown around a
shaved skull and the samurai warriors, dragons and koi
fish of the Japanese full body tattoo.

•

The emptiness that Ava felt was the emptiness a clean
canvas might feel waiting for the caress of an artist's
brush. She knew she could never use religion to fill that
emptiness. She had tried drugs in high school, but found
they made her feel stupid and out of control. She liked
an order to everything and thought underachieving was
overrated. During college, she had used sex to fill the
emptiness. Those encounters, with dumb handsome boys
only, created parallel universes of emptiness. She had
never liked their clumsy fingers, the way they reached for
her, squeezed her, tested to see if she were *ready*.

•

After each desperate encounter with dumb handsome
boys, Ava rewarded herself with a tattoo and redesigned
her body. She started slowly and secretly. A crescent
moon above the ankle, a thin ribbon of triangles across
her wrist, easily hidden under a watch or bracelet.

Seven Sentences Set in Hogan's Bar & Grill

I

At the trial of a man accused of stabbing to death a fellow patron of Hogan's Bar & Grill, witnesses testified that they never thought the defendant, a former child actor most famous for his uncredited role as 'boy kidnapped by clown,' would settle an argument about holiday television specials with violence.

2

Police were called, once again, to Hogan's Bar & Grill to break up a melee between a famous philosopher from Copenhagen reciting the Periodic Table and regular patrons responding with angry quotations from Sartre, Camus and Nietzsche.

3

After a long vacation in Amsterdam, where a member of our tour offered an undercover police officer oral sex for 6 Euros and a pack of black market cigarettes, we patronized Hogan's Bar & Grill only to find ourselves embroiled in an argument regarding underwear, Letters-to-the-Editor and scratch ticket wins.

4

In the backroom, by the pool table and jukebox, of Hogan's Bar & Grill, to which I had withdrawn in order to avoid Lou Hogan's glare every time I ordered a sparkling water, with no lemon or lime – my stomach had been acting up and I felt no need to inform Lou of my malady – a fellow patron, who I had noticed once or twice when he received a volley of abuse from the regulars after he had selected soft rock songs from the '70s on the jukebox, told me he was the last living member of a construction crew remodeling a brownstone who had discovered, behind the walnut wainscoting of a back hallway that led to a bricked up door, playing cards manufactured with a material they had never seen, or touched, depicting obscene images and extraterrestrial hieroglyphics.

5

We never found out who left the rusty torpedo leaning against the wall in the breezeway behind Hogan's Bar & Grill until the kitchen sink anarchist and maladroit heir to a haversack manufacturing empire, who, every after-noon, took a seat near the men's room and placed an old typewriter on the table, but was never seen to hit any of the keys, except the return and space bar just so he could, we assumed, listen to the bell while he drank a single gin and tonic with a slice of lemon that he chewed on while muttering about half-eaten puppets, burning effigies constructed out of napkins and radioactive submarines.

6

A great ape tutor and handler, famous for her mentoring a chimpanzee midwife, who excelled at every event held at Hogan's Bar & Grill, whether it was karaoke night on Thursday, quiz night on Friday or open-mic on Saturday, admitted that, as a young girl, she had accidentally knelt on a baby gerbil and crushed its head.

7

The first thing we noticed about the rocketship perched on the roof of Hogan's Bar & Grill was its small size, like a VW bus decked out in alien peace symbols, webbed in light, rocking as if at sea.

The Beatles Agnostics

George was never my favorite Beatle, my co-worker said.

Yea, but what about "While My Guitar Gently Weeps?" I said.

I'll give you that one. And the other one. I know it wasn't a Beatles song.

"My Sweet Lord," I said.

Yea, that one. The one where he ripped off another song, wasn't it.

I remember as kids, I said, running through the breeze-way and there'd always be that older boy who'd carried a knife and he'd cut a pimple ball in half so we could play stick ball. And those fucking cars making us stop just so's they'd drive by. Making faces at the driver and us throwing shit at the car as it drove away, waiting for the taillights to go on cause then you'd know the driver'd get out and chase us down the street. But we knew all the shortcuts and alleys and garage roofs we could hop up on. Then some other boy'd grab an old mop handle and run through the backyards smacking all the laundry down off the lines. Someone's radio'd be playing and "Michelle" would come on the AM station. You know, one of the ones McCartney always sang.

He's my least favorite Beatle, my co-worker said.

Me too, I said, but it was the only time I ever heard someone speaking French, except for the Canadians upstairs. She was always bleh bleh blah we we way bleh bleh blue. He almost never said a word, but when he did all he'd ever say was taste a war taste a war taste a war.

What's a war taste like? my co-worker said.

I dunno. But I always liked that song, "Michelle."

Scenes from a Commute

1

The mother on the bus, who gave her squalling teething baby a Zippo lighter to chew on, highlighted alternating passages in Boswell's *Life of Samuel Johnson* with pink, green and yellow markers.

2

Basking in the relative silence between trains, while the busker tuned up, a woman stepped closer to the edge of infinity.

3

There were moments during his daily commute when a man felt nervous as if his daydreams of becoming an active shooter had evolved.

4

In hindsight, he expected a phrenological exam from the woman with yellow cotton candy stuck in her hair. He did not, however, expect her to charge so much for her services.

Hagiography of Kafka

I am, you said, transmogrified from beetle to person,
from house to tree, from dog to cat, from bird to bee.

Okay, I said, shuffling eggs and mushrooms and a
pepper from the garden around a frying pan, everybody
has something, some burden, some secret history. In the
end, we're all just trying to get through the heatwave.

Heatwave, you said, let me tell you about heatwaves,
about thunder storms and lightning strikes, sewers
overflowing and *enterococcus* at the beach. Let me tell you
about parasites and humans, mosquitoes and beetles.

Always with the beetles, I said.

Have you looked in the mirror, you said. Have you
looked up the definition of hexapod. Are you pushing
eggs around a frying pan or nibbling on a leaf that only
tastes like a Spanish omelet.

Hagiography of Magellan

We could stand in the middle of the road and build a house together, I said, or, we could drive to the shore and see where the ocean carries us.

We could hop a freight to McDonalds, you said, and dip our fries in a strawberry shake and wait for the waves to wash away the parking lot and carry us back down the tracks.

We could read new books and burn the old ones, I said, and from the ashes of this bonfire of vocabularies a new ink is mixed and mortared and new words on new paper are written.

We could block out the sun, magnify the moon, you said, or estimate the day and hour and minute when the Hadron Collider rips gravity out of space and restores balance to the tides.

We could, I said, stand in the middle of the road and, like Magellan before us, circumnavigate our world just by touching fingers and lips.

We should, you said.

Ötzi

Find my killer, Ötzi, the iceman said.

But I want to tattoo you, Ava said. I want to feel inside your fur hat and wear your leggings. I want to kiss the rabbet left behind by the arrow that killed you.

Find my killer. That's all I ask, Ötzi said.

But we could circumnavigate the universe, become cartographers of each other's bodies. Spend languorous afternoons under an equatorial sun, our skin an electric current.

I'll give you berries and nuts if you find my killer, Ötzi said.

Before I find your killer, I want to find out why he tracked you and chased you up that mountain. Where did you live? Who did you offend or trespass against? What gods did you worship?

When you find my killer, Ötzi said, you'll know the truth. Until then I'll remain an enigma machine, a code to be broken, an amorphous black hole of unmatched DNA, tattoos and longing.

Urban Renewal

I

We hopped freights to go down the line for McDonalds.

2

We were a conspiracy of poets and delinquents drinking
the coldest water from a bubbler in the city yards.

3

During the day, the big kids palmed us quarters and
dimes to use our sting rays to make drug runs.

4

We knew freedom running along the roofs of abandoned
buildings, the squeak of sneakers as we spread our version
of urban renewal.

5

We asked so little of gravity as we jimmied the factory's
elevator door open and edged along a greasy precipice.

6

From the Coast Guard station the sea sweeps out to the
edge of the world. We rode our bikes fifteen miles along a
potholed highway how much further could Nova Scotia be?

———

Letters to Travel Agencies

1

The brochure did not mention panhandling poltergeists.
However, we enjoyed the alien abduction.

2

A man sat in the corner of our room throughout our stay.
He never moved day or night and when he spoke it was
in a language that consisted solely of computer-like beeps
and burps.

3

The pathways to the beach, paved with crushed porcelain
doll parts, exceeded our expectations.

4

While knowledgeable, our tour guide's insistence that he
was just a patsy proved unnerving to the older members
of our group.

5

An intern came to the hotel lobby and asked if anyone
would like to dismantle alien spacecraft stored in hangers
carved out of Antarctic ice.

6

It came as a surprise to us that not only did we need a visa to visit the People's Republic of X, customs agents required us to recite the Periodic Tables.

An Ostrich Feather and Three Gold Watch Fobs

Buried behind horse-hair plaster these magic time
capsules left a grimy black dust on our clothes and skin –
who knows what it did to our lungs. Opening the walls
we felt like archaeologists, crossing a span of millennia
in just over a century. We were Schliemanns discovering
Troy all over again, proving Homer was a historian just as
Herodotus claimed to be. The stud cavities were insulated
with newspapers that melted in our hands like so many
desiccated bones of heroes turned to black dust. Later, all
that history washed off in the shower and we were back to
feeling like hagiographers making up history as we went
along, each piece of splintery lathe a new fiction.

Something About Talking Animals

Under normal circumstances owls do not talk, but when the boy brought home a talking owl, his parents said the boy could not keep the owl.

But I eat mice, the owl said.

So do cats and you don't hear them talking, the boy's father said.

The next day, the boy brought home a talking cat as a companion for his talking owl.

And so it went until the house had become a zoo of talking animals.

Has anyone seen my parents, the boy said.

Postcards from a Parallel Universe

I

I left a dish on the hotel nightstand tiled with coins from seven countries for the cleaning maid.

2

We allowed our senses to be defiled by the tranquil beauty and brilliancy of the ocean's skin.

3

On Sunday, I drove to the bootlegger's house and sat in his living room staining the ceiling with nicotine and watching the wallpaper peel.

4

The sun was too hot. We sat on the veranda and listened to Nietzsche on the wireless, as if the agony of the horse in Turin, the certain failure of his sanity had eclipsed the dancing, the crushing weight of three dimensions and the tyranny of high expectations.

5

Snow scrubbed away the bitter moon while children scattered rock salt on the lawn.

6

We sat in the parlor eating apples and drinking chai tea for supper while the night doppler shifted the sound of cars and trucks, a wash of rock kelp in a tidal pool, a rumble of boots.

Stratospheric Microwaves Are No Cure for Acne

Colman convinced himself that gluing buffalo head nickels to manhole covers was an artistic endeavor. If only his father would see it that way. Colman reasoned that mixing the epoxy required a special technique, one that he learned from trial and error. How many times had he come away with a forefinger attached to a thumb. Only a painful tearing of skin could loosen them. His father might suggest dousing the hand in lacquer thinner, but Colman knew that that was his father's solution for everything. A second degree burn: lacquer thinner. A mosquito bite: lacquer thinner. In the end, the Electric Avenue Neighborhood Watch found Colman's nickel gluing unsavory, unsanitary and unacceptable by every community standard it consulted. After his arrest, Colman's parents finally entered his room and discovered the true depth of their son's artistic vision. They soon realized that the room's doorway was the weak link to his tinfoil lined sanctuary.

We found secret messages on cereal boxes, in fields of
freshly mown hay, in the damp chill of the bay as we
watched the Perseids, in our wishes spilled on the ground,
in box elder beetles, in extraterrestrial horticultural
manuals, in the fibers of a daddy long legs' web, in the
scribblings of circus clowns and poets and three card
monte hustlers, in the mossy rindles of a sidewalk, on
the faces of oblong asteroids, in the patterns and layers
of shoveled volcanic ash, from the static of a pirate radio
transmission, on the face of a beech tree infested with
scale and infected with *nectria*, in the chem trail of a rocket
ship, inked on our bodies and no longer subject to
interpretation.

A Secret History of Acadia

At a bed & breakfast, on the Fundy shore, where the owner, wearing only a housecoat, served toasted homemade bread with strawberry jam and, when fog did not glaze the bay, we saw seagulls pursuing whales and fishing boats chumming, a disheveled guest told us, in strictest confidence, he said, the Princess of Acadia had murdered the Prince and was last seen living on the beach near Digby Gut where the RCMP decided to wait her out and see what the tides brought in.

We followed the trace down the cliff, where smugglers had once kicked aside prosauropod bones, the weight of glaciers down their necks, tides abraded the shore to salted basalt and granite and shale and red sandstone, each stratum dangerous, each pointing to the littoral hideout of the Princess where the blue spruce forests stumbled over the cliffs retreating to the sea from the bogs and eskers, the blood red fields of blueberry, the caribou plains and granite boulders planted atop each other like a giant's toy, precarious in the fog.

At the edge of the shore, the smell of an ebbing tide and a herd of grey seals hauled out on the beach mingled with a hurling ocean, a line of rain become an elongated and rusty smudge like a cut nail dropped in the beach grass. This is where the glaciers stopped, where the horses are always running, their manes washing away the continent.

A Secret History of Existentialism

The existentialist from Essex understood the history of
boat building and fried clams, the theory behind golden
battered onion rings and a rational existence despite an
irrational universe, but he fretted over salt marshes and
Le Grand Dérangement of the Acadians, of the supremacy
of great whites over grey seals, of sperm whales battering
ships, of the futility of memory, and of time and history
reset, as if trading green stamps for furniture or a crock
pot never used, or a display lamp with a bulb that
flickered and smoked, a pocket calculator turned upside
down always reading ⅂⅂Ǝℎ negated a mackerel sky
showering missiles and rockets.

A Secret History of Exorcism

When the door to door exorcist arrived, we let him in before he had a chance to introduce himself. At first, he stood in the hallway as if testing the space for satanic residue. Satisfied, the door to door exorcist ventured in to the kitchen. We offered him coffee and a snack, but he declined and moved toward the dining room. It was in that room that he realized he was in the wrong house. We insisted he stay for dinner.

A Secret History of Kahoutek

We broke in to condemned factories and lit fires. At
night, the stars resembled a sluice of dead light fractured
and emitting a hum we heard through broken windows.
Kahoutek looked like a dirty smudge in the rake of blue
light from the patrol cars.

A Secret History of the Solar System

We came upon a trio of unicyclists riding abreast down the street. A bus, full of agitated passengers, strained behind the threesome. The world tilted as if a ship at sea yawed to port and the unicyclists danced over the pavement with each other. We felt nothing. It was not an earthquake. The bus stopped at a red light. My fingers traced hot and cold trajectories across your stomach. Above us the stars pinwheeled while asteroids tumbled.

A Secret History of Woodworking

Behind a workbench faced with flinty homasote and tiled with auger bits, clamps, and pencil nubs, I found a city lit by bioluminescence, ships circumnavigating the ocean by touch, a forest of old growth walnut and elm, shipwrights and cabinetmakers at lunch talking shit and sharpening chisels.

Secret Moments in the Lives of the Famous

I

Surrounded by young street urchins, Igor Stravinsky watched through a hole in the fence. The players swatted and threw in syncopated semi-quavers, followed by a rest then another frenzied burst. Baseball had returned to the form he liked best: *molto allegro*.

2

Ernest Hemingway never noticed the hieroglyphics behind the pegboard in his basement workshop until a water-stained piece had broken off. Removing the tools and baby food jars of assorted screws and nails, he dismantled the moldering pegboard and set it on the cement floor. He brushed away skeins of saw-dusted cobweb. He thought of calling his wife to show her, but she never understood his tinkering.

3

Henry David Thoreau woke to the sound of a frumpy amphibian fussing about in his room. The lizard creature with sausage-like claws struggled to pick up the small objects that littered his desk: a pencil, a piece of wood that he had whittled to pick his teeth with, a saucer tiled with coins and assorted scraps of paper embellished by scribblings that he had jotted down when his mind vacillated between stupor and moments of clarity.

4

While out walking, Myrna Loy found a dead rabbit on
a section of the bike path still under construction. The
routinely ignored detour signs, large upturned orange
barrels, and solar powered highway signs warning drivers
away from the curbless sidewalk never kept the rabbit
safe. The next morning Myrna left a half dozen Granny
Smith apples. By the afternoon, they were gone and the
trace that led to the banks of the river held only muddy
secrets, animal tracks and a plastic bag unable to free itself
from history.

5

While cleaning up the cigarettes ground into a rug and
the dry, sticky ponds on the kitchen floor in her New York
apartment, Bette Davis wished she were back in California
lounging on Black's Beach, eating fruit and drinking
Singapore Slings with a handsome sailor.

6

Norman Mailer never told anyone that he enjoyed the
smell of a new car. For him, that flabby fragrance of
ozone had just enough ethyl formate ester to make him
hunger for a stiff drink.

7

A stack of soiled playing cards in his letter box caused
Shemp Howard to look over his shoulder and reconsider
the story he had cooked up to tell his wife when she
questioned him about the stain on his lapel.

8

While at the library, Joan Crawford rarely checked out
a book. Instead, she wandered the stacks of rare books,
running her manicured and lacquered fingers along the
spines, inhaling that musty, erotic smell of old paper and
leather boards.

9

Tennessee Williams attributed the plague of flashing
lights, multi-colored streamers and shrill noises to the
"sauce." Only later, while traveling abroad, did he read
about failed weather balloon experiments, rocket circuitry
malfunctions and distracted sonarmen.

10

Ava Gardner dreamt about the shadowed history of
humans rubbing red ochre on the bodies of their dead,
of pushing dye into skin by tapping it with oak needles.
Long before humans painted on the walls of caves Ava
realized that skin was the first canvas artists worked on.

11

Fred MacMurray never wondered why his dinner guests always excused themselves just as he began his post-prandial busking.

12

Whenever the washing machine in the basement lurched into the spin cycle, George Sanders employed mind control techniques he learned on the set of *All About Eve* to block out the infernal screeching.

Alien Spacecraft

We agreed to dismantle the alien spacecraft in our neighbor's yard. Not that they had accused us of building it in the first place. In the winter, I shovel snow from their sidewalk, so why not take apart a spacecraft. Our neighbors are elderly and living with a silver saucer the size of a small school bus at that age struck me as a cruel and unusual joke.

At first, everyone in the neighborhood pitched in when they could. But then the excuses came: activities, dental appointments, migraines. I suspect the real reason remained simpler. Our tools had done nothing to penetrate the exterior of the spacecraft. The damn thing was too well built.

We eventually called in a neighbor's friend who owned welding equipment. The amateur welder stood in the backyard and looked at the spacecraft for ten minutes before circumnavigating it. While round the back, he leaned down and sniffed at the shiny metal.

If I touch this with any arc or flame, he said. I'll blow the whole neighborhood to high hell.

I called the city, but they told me they had no means with which to dispose of a spacecraft. NASA and the Air Force never returned my calls.

Our neighbor's great-grandchildren play on the damn thing. Every time they slide off and bruise a knee or an elbow, it heals within an hour and they're back climbing on the spacecraft. When it rains, the ship becomes a silvery waterslide. Conversely, it's never hot to the touch in the sun and seems to cool the kids if they get overheated.

I hope the extraterrestrial occupants come back soon. It is unclear how an alien spacecraft might affect property values in the neighborhood.

An Alien Encounter

What if, the boy said to his parents, what if I build a spaceship.

Out of what, the boy's father said.

From meteorites and platinum and seaborgium.

How will you pay for this spaceship, the boy's father said.

With my keno winnings and hustling down at the pool hall, with craps in the back alley behind school.

You have such a vivid imagination, the boy's mother said.

What if, the boy said to his parents, what if there is a spaceship already here to take me back to my home planet.

I gave birth to you, I nursed you, I bled for you, the boy's mother said.

Did you, the boy said, did you.

Broken Window

A broken window was proof enough for Bill that messages he received on the shortwave radio set were extraterrestrial.

Kids, Bill's neighbor, Jerry, said.

I'm not so sure. Bill said. Kids don't understand that technology.

Do you own a gun? I would if I were you.

This is bigger than weaponry. I don't wanna say dark forces, but...

Dark forces always come locked and loaded, Jerry said. Extra water and batteries can't hurt.

Batteries won't do any good. All neutralized at the end, Bill said.

Both men looked through the window as if its shattered geometry was a map to a decaying Universe where Black Holes foretold the Apocalypse.

Kids, Jerry said.

Where's the baseball? Where's the rock? I don't agree, Bill said.

Sneaky. Kids today know things we only learned as adults.

I'm telling you, this goes beyond knowledge.

Bill pried a dagger of glass from the window pane. He

———

handed the piece to Jerry who examined it, turning it

over, searching for clues from every angle. He ran the acuminated edge along his thumb, scoring the skin, but not drawing blood.

We're talking end of the world as we know it, Bill said.

My advice then: plywood and extra water, Jerry said.

The one-handed alienist rarely offered advice. There exists, he said, in the pot on the stove, a hidden mystery, algebra and alchemy come to life.

If there is a secret to the universe, then that must be it, I said.

No, the alienist said, the secret to the universe lies with one-handed juggling, hanging wallpaper while sailing across the ocean, pulling the pin on a grenade and scrawling anagrams on the walls of an asbestos-lined factory.

The alienist held up his damaged hands, scar tissue where the four fingers on his right hand once pointed leaving only a useless thumb and the left hand missing it's thumb as if some demented member of an anti-opposable thumb cult had performed surgery with table saw precision. In fact, it was the alienist that had performed the operation. The four fingers by accident on a saw and later justifying cutting his thumb off with an axe saying it felt unbalanced with two thumbs and only one hand fully populated with fingers. How he held the axe with the fingerless hand he reveals to no one.

The alienist said, how can we master the weather? If a tornado touches down and like a felt tip marker blackens the earth, what are we supposed to say? It was God's will. Shit happens. If a boy comes home from school and finds his parents having sex, does this boy suddenly

remember the taste and touch of his mother's breast? If carpenters remodeling a brownstone find a wooden box filled with coded messages hidden behind horse hair plaster and lathe, do we search their houses only to find each one empty and scrubbed clean?

It's all chaos, I said.

Then why aren't we pinballing through space? The Earth bouncing off Mars and Venus and back out to Jupiter, racking up points each time our planet takes out a moon. Europa is a thousand points, Io 750 points, Thelxinoe just 10 points.

Gravity holds the chaos at bay, I said.

Gravity didn't hold my fingers together. Gravity dropped them to the floor as fast as a penny dropped from the top of the Empire State Building, or Evelyn McHale, an angel sent to punish the gravity deniers. But gravity is the avenging angel. Wicked gravity, just like that Jim Carroll song, people always falling from east two nine.

Memory Illuminated

The sour paving stones beneath his feet no longer
illuminated the path as if, in the dimness, memories
of light and the car accident that killed his mother and
launched him to relative safety eluded him.

At the Fisherman's Feast of the Madonna Del Soccorso di Sciacca

A boy said to his friend, I saw alien dervishes, rocket ship captains, deep sea divers, underground filmmakers, poets and carpenters.

I discussed crime and publishing and anarchy with four Charlies: Ponzi, Bukowski, Chaplin and Manson, the friend said.

I smelled molasses and rising seas.

If the seas rise we should line a cement bin with rubber and sail to Newfoundland.

Why Newfoundland, why not Greenland, or Iceland.

In Newfoundland, the friend said, we could fish the Flemish Cap from dories, stringing out our lines for cod and haddock.

Why fish the Flemish Cap, a boy said to his friend, when we could plunder Vinland all over again.

The Tourists

1

A boy fell out of the top bunk and split open his head.
The boy's mother didn't know what to do so she went
across the street to the travel agency and booked a flight
to an exotic locale. When she returned, the boy's mother
gave him a Boeing 707 model and made sure the boy
never fell asleep again.

2

We stopped for lunch. Rain showers passed through and
left us searching for ladders, stairs, ropes, anything to let
us climb back down from our pedestals. You threw me on
the hood of the car and kissed me.

3

They found a whale carcass and hid a vertebrae in the
trunk when they crossed the border. There was marrow
inside the bone, but they didn't mind that ocean smell.

The Weathermen

Look at weather this morning? Ciaran said.

We're fine here, Nick said. Doppler radar showed clear.

Not down South.

We're not down South. We're fine here. All day.

That's got to be hell on earth down there, Ciaran said.

Nick positioned a bundle of shingles on his right shoulder and followed Ciaran up the ladder and onto the roof.

We get bad weather, too, Nick said.

Ciaran straddled the peak of the roof and slit open a bundle of shingles with his utility knife. Not like that. Not like that at all. Your man said three people died from a tornado.

From the peak of the roof, Nick could see the city spread east to the harbor and the ocean. He counted the islands in the harbor, but could not smell the ocean. There was only tar paper heating up in the sun, the shingles getting softer as the sun climbed.

Ever tell you that my grandfather was a tin can sailor? I like those words, Nick said. Tin cans.

What the fuck you on about? Ciaran said.

My grandfather served on a destroyer. They called them tin cans. He survived the largest naval battle in history.

His ship sank. Drifted in the water for two days before being rescued. By then half the men had gone under.

Half of how many? Ciaran said.

I don't know. They were attacked by sharks, drank salt water, exhausted. You can't blame them if they just let go.

Sharks. Fuck that, Ciaran said.

I know. Sharks. You don't even see them.

Nick smelled the air changing and tasted iron, the ozone charging. To the west, cumulonimbus clouds clawed and struggled to mass, a looming, rumbling wall that crept east. Nick looked back at the harbor and realized he might have counted one of the smaller islands twice.

Thought we were good for the day, Ciaran said.

We are. For the most part.

Nick and Ciaran worked until the first drops of rain sputtered down on them. They pulled the blue tarp tight and battened it down with pieces of strapping.

Let's stay on the roof until this thing blows over.

They counted intervals between the lightning and thunder. The doppler radar had lied.

Ciaran looked at him. I'm counting six seconds.

I lost count, Nick said.

Storm Coming Up The Bay

Storm coming up the bay doesn't
stop us from going out, sea
nothing but whitecaps. I'm in
the bow of the 12-foot outboard,
my great Uncle in the stern,
steering, gunwale barely above
the waves soaking him, turns
into a trough and a wave
comes over, the cold water
rushing up from the Atlantic,
from the Bay of Fundy,
from Baie Ste. Marie baptizes
me and at age 13 I have my
first real taste of the sea, and
the salt got inside my veins
and it won't dry out. The ocean
calms me. Tasted the saltwater
of three oceans, weathered
hurricanes, typhoons and monsoons,
withstood 50-foot tides, 30-foot
waves, and still I go back
because the ocean calms me from
manic storms, from depression
swells rolling to shore, tsunamis
and rogue waves. We finished,
my great Uncle and me, that afternoon
on the bay jigging for mackerel and

also caught a fat pollack that my
gran-pére refuses to clean and cook.
Worms, he says, that fish is full
of worms. My gran-mére is not happy
I walk into her house soaking wet,
but she is happy her brother made
me wear the life jacket. The
mackerel will taste good with new
potatoes and carrots and the next
day at Mass, my gran-mére will pray
for my safety and I'll pray to a
different god, to go back to sea,
even if, for now, it's only the fog
smothered coast of Nova Scotia.

Thirst

A pick-up truck, its bed filled with ice stippled with bottles of water, stopped in front of our houses. We let the children go out and take as many bottles of water as they could carry and drink at the same time. But one boy and girl, offspring of the family of mimes who lived two doors down, held back. Finally, after all the other children had quenched their thirst, the boy took a single bottle of water and brought it to his sister. She poured the water onto the sidewalk and then the two of them proceeded to drink from the empty bottle, passing it between each other as if they were hobos sharing a bottle of muscatel.

My Old Captain Died Yesterday

He went to the beach
to meditate and nap
while the ocean he loved
kept up its ceaseless energy,
its need to touch and
taste everything
especially death.

The old man lived two doors down died.

The old man lived
two doors down died.
I always shoveled the
sidewalk front of his house.
I'd see him in his
front porch, cigarette
in one hand, oxygen
bottle in the other.
We'd talk a while told
me his old man built
the front porches on
our brick rowhouses.
As a kid, he worked on
the small farm where
the housing project is
now rounding up the
stray animals before
they wandered on to the
train tracks. Only thing
he ever said about the
war was he was glad he
got wounded on Peleliu,
saved him from fighting
on Okinawa. Can tell
you were in the service,
he said. Got that look
of a guy who's seen things.

Nothing like you, nothing
like a shitty volcanic
rock in the middle of
the ocean with no real
strategic value that I
sailed past and only
knew as a name on a ship.
Worst I ever saw was
inside of a Filipino jail cell.
That's more than some of
these no-good-niks, he said,
like my lazy grandson.
The old man's dead now and
his lazy grandson can
shovel his own sidewalk.

Reincarnation

My mother said in her past life she was a gamekeeper, but she refused to say which animals were in her care. I imagined it did not end well. There was a rush of fear on my mother's face when I asked what happened.

My father claimed he had no past lives. He had many lives and after each death my father reanimated himself and found a new vocation. It was better, he said, not to work in the job that killed you. That way your only risk becomes a challenge to master a new trade.

I was too young to remember past lives and not old enough to die working in this trade or that vocation. So, I sat and listened to my parents mutter and cough and sneak into the bathroom together when they thought I was asleep.

Lucy the Magdalene Requiem

Lucy the Magdalene worked at a cafe in Ocean Beach. Married a sailor, she would tell customers who asked. Make-up barely covered the bruises on her face. Every night he would bring home his buddies. In the morning after he left for the base, Lucy cleaned up the sticky puddles of puke and beer, and vacuumed out cigarette ashes ground into the carpet. This was not the America she expected, or the America she deserved.

Lucy didn't recognize me at first. Swimming naked at the beach, and the family cooking a dog, I said. Her eyes smiled and a shadow of happiness flared across her face.

I'm getting out of the Navy and heading back East, I said.

Married a sailor, she said. He's stationed on the base, so no WESTPAC for him, no Filipina bar girls for him, she said, trying to laugh.

What I didn't tell, what I wished I told her was I wanted to take her with me, to show her a real America, of watching the sun set on the plains and turning around to watch the moon rise, of standing where the watersheds divide and feeling the continent spreading away, of sleeping in Frank Lloyd Wright designed motels where I would trace a map of the day's travels on her body, of swimming in each of the five Great Lakes and the Atlantic Ocean.

Instead, I ordered a grilled cheese sandwich with a slice of tomato and our fingers touched when Lucy handed me the change and for a moment we both felt electric back in Subic Bay, back under the vampire Christ crucifix in her room and the sheet lightening and the jungle and hot sweltering nights in the clubs on Magsaysay Boulevard.

I left Lucy in that cafe, a sadness rising as she refilled condiment bottles and thought about back home in the Philippines where another birthday for President Marcos united the country.

Later, I found out, Lucy went home and left her sailor husband a note and walked out the quarter mile down the pier at the end of Newport Avenue, out on the right arm of the pier, and in the thickening fog, Lucy the Magdalene took off her clothes, climbed the rail and dove in, a perfect creature returning to the sea.

Medals

We didn't get a medal for rescuing the Vietnamese boat people crowded in a leaking, shattered scow in the South China Sea. We took them onboard and gave them blankets, water, food, medical attention. But they were yesterday's news, cast off and cast away. We did get a medal for rescuing Japanese fishermen off Samoa after their trawler sank. We spent day and half looking for heads floating in the water as if scanning for coconuts, wet, black-haired tips of icebergs, sharks feeding below, sun scorching above. From a crew of sixteen we pulled less than half out of the ocean. For that they gave us a medal.

Thank You for Your Service

Hung myself till I blacked out.
The bowline knot came undone and
any safe harbor I had sought beyond
this world had left me adrift and
cast off on the floor, wretched,
drowning the sun in
the sweet mystery of the sea,
always wrestling with death,
always for hate's sake,
always Melville –
never far from a Greylock
on the horizon,
breaching like a whale,
        white?

In the darkened ship,
haunted as the cord dangled,
useless and misspent,
I fell off the edge of the world,
swallowed by sea monsters.

Woke up with a neck board pushing against my swollen
throat – someone will find the irony in struggling to
breathe – the sour smell of the ambulance, then the
florescent hell of the emergency room, a guard outside
the room as if I was contagion infecting the sane.

Nurse prepping me for x-rays,
CAT scans, psych ward, says:
"I heard you were a veteran. Thank you for your service."

*Veteran is a Caucasian M with a h/o bipolar II most recent
episode depressed, s/p recent SA in 12/2014, polysubstance
use disorder (alcohol, opiate, amphetamine, hallucinogens) in
remission and chronic migraines who presents for follow-up. He
has symptoms consistent with bipolar spectrum illness, including
periods of hypomania with grandiosity, impulsivity and racing
thoughts and severe periods of depression with suicidal ideation,
since his teenage years.*

On the ward
they let us out in a courtyard
each day for twenty minutes to walk,
to run if we wished,
but not hop over the fence.
The courtyard sat on top of a
parking garage and
below it hard-hatted men
worked, reinforcing concrete.

In the courtyard, there was the woman
who always sidled up to me but never said anything —

---

dissociative?
damaged?

I could see in her eyes
the way the blue flickered
off and on,
off and on
as if an old style light switch,
round and puckered
in a grimy switch plate,
had been pushed,
sounding with a determined
thunk and the light,
taking a moment to cross
a universe
where comets and stars disappear,
shined because it had
died so very long ago.

*Routine record review and consultation with providers indicates
Veteran remains at high-risk for suicide and/or suicidal bx's.
Veteran will remain on High Risk flag list until next review
period - 90 days. Veteran continues to present with ongoing
symptoms of depression, grandiosity, impulsivity, racing
thoughts, and increased irritability in the context of various life
stressors and endorses transient SI, without plan or intent.*

My neck remained swollen and
bruised from the electrical cord and
my voice become a perfect baritone honey.
All my other careers failed,
so why not a new one in radio.

On the ward
there was the guy who copied me,
trying to prove he was as crazy,
as pained, as depressed.
But he did have a better voice and
told the group he checked himself
in because his girl friend
told him he needed help.

She probably wanted him
out of the house so she could
fuck a real man and not a guy
who said he got angry when he
tried to write a song and
always got one of the notes wrong
as if a semi-quaver had slipped
off the page and spilled on the
floor and the dog had licked it up.

But he only said this during
group after I mentioned
that I wrote soundtrack music.
He was like that.
Copying me.

———

Even down to my inflections when,
during group,
we took turns reading some
aspirational aphorisms and
me reading them like
I was already auditioning
for that new job in radio.

Pt experienced SI with plan to drown himself, but no intent,
while walking by a river. Pt stated he was able to manage SI, by
reminding himself that it was just a thought and using cognitive
restructuring. He also told himself that if he was still experiencing
SI by the time he got home, he would call the Veterans Crisis Line
and/or present for emergency services.

Out in the courtyard
the guy always copying me
walked in slow circles
as if the depression how-to manual
told him that you do
everything slower when
you're depressed.
But not me.
I get cranky when I'm depressed.
I get cranky when I'm manic.
I walked my usual brisk pace,
counter clockwise going against the
normal flow of the rest of the patients.

———

When the damaged woman sidled up to me,
walking the same direction,
the poseur reversed his direction,
but kept to his agonized pace.
We lapped him and later in group
this guy said he wanted the
golf courses to be open all winter.
In New England!?

That's why he felt melancholy?
That's why I tried to hang myself?
That's why the damaged woman always sidled up to me?

Mood was mildly dysthymic, and affect was full and appropriate.
Pt was alert throughout the session and oriented x3. Pt's speech
was normal with respect to rhythm and rate. Thought processes
were normal and coherent with no evidence of distorted or
psychotic symptoms.

On the ward,
I shared a little bedroom
with a roommate who sobbed
all night because the shock therapy
was not working for him and
he kept sitting there,
          staring,
as if an airborne event
had gone nuclear and

———

the jittery winter light
slanting through the dusty
blinds had scraped clean his eyes.
Veteran has historical and biological risk factors that place him
at a chronic, moderate risk for SI and SDV. Based on his current
presentation, absence of SI, and no hospitalizations in the past
90 days Veteran does not present as acute or high risk for suicide
at this time. Category I PRF - High Risk for Suicide will be
inactivated.

On the ward,
I played Scrabble,
with missing tiles,
with two college girls
burdened by mid-term
workloads and abstruse
rituals of sexual identity.
One of the women jumped up
from the table when she scored
fifty points and performed a
little jig and slapped her thigh,
counted her fingers,
slapped her other thigh,
counted the other hand's fingers and,
once more,
danced a two-step shuffle
before sitting down and
counting all the fingers on both hands.
It seemed a breakthrough.

———

The depression poseur, looked over at us
            — jealous?
as he pretended to scribble in his journal,
his record of mental illness.
Jealous that I was a veteran with tattoos?
Jealous that college girls played Scrabble with me?
Jealous that the staff therapists liked me?
Jealous that a sub-verbal woman sidled up to me?

He kept dropping hints in group
that he looked forward to
electroshock therapy.
It would be like a badge,
a medal he never got because
he never served and
no one would ever thank him
for his service.
Every time he saw an orderly, or a doctor
thank me for my service,
he seemed to glare,
or, that's what I thought.
My depression had
made me paranoid
            — I have the medals to prove it.

Reviewed emergency procedures in case SI increases in frequency or intensity, including calling the Veterans Crisis Line, presenting to the BR or WRX ERs, or calling 911. Pt was amenable to using these resources if needed.

When the poseur
came back from his
electro shock session
he no longer appeared
jealous because
I had tried to hang myself
or that the damaged woman
always sidled up to me.
He didn't come out of his room
the rest of the day and
when he finally did,
he looked like my roommate,
volleys of electricity inside
his head trying to make 50 point
words with only vowels,
but missing all the E tiles.

*We continued to explore thoughts and feelings related to
Veteran's suicide attempt and chronic passive ideation, including
the function that suicidality may currently serve for him. Veteran
expressed comfort in the belief that "I always have the option of
suicide in my back pocket." We explored the benefits and draw-
backs to this relationship with suicide, including ways in which it
may interfere with his ability to fully engage with the world.*

When I walked out
of the ward and
into a post-suicide world

still thinking that somehow
I had succeeded and
that all this was limbo,
some demented purgatory
where I had to continue living
my life even though
I had killed myself,
the nurse who checked me
out, again,
thanked me for my service.

This is what you say to a person who is dying
for my brother Marc

Not:

You've lived a full life.
You have a caring soul,
You'll get into Heaven somehow
You'll soon be with ...
Mama
Papa
An older sibling
A tragically killed sibling
Who died too young,
A favorite Aunt
Your old angry creepy
Uncle who hated
Blacks and Jews and Catholics
Your first dog –
Mine was named Sparky –

Not:

Did you know I carry a
Razor blade in my wallet?
I stole from you once.
I kissed your wife,
Your husband,
Your daughter,
Your son,

Your grandmother.
I wrote that note about you,
Lying that you were a liar
And a thief when,
It reality it was me.
I bet you didn't know I lie and steal?

Not:

Did I ever tell you
I heard a black-capped chickadee
Thonk against a window, went outside
and found it on the ground.
I picked the bird up and held it
In my palm until the bird
Woke up, looked at me,
Looked around, and
Sat there, for several minutes,
Collecting its thoughts.
Then the black-capped chickadee
Flew off and I felt like I
Finally did something good.
Do you know if birds get concussions?
I put the rat poison
In your dog's food.
Wasn't his name Sparky,
I can't remember.

Not:

They faked the conspiracy
About the fake moon landing.
Did you know they have a cure
For what's killing you, but your
Doctor won't make any money and
The insurance companies don't
Care whether you live or die?
Do you think climate change
Is causing all the raining
And burning
And flooding?
You won't be around
When the asteroid they
Just landed a probe on
Hits the earth.
Did you know they think
Life came riding in on
An asteroid?
I wonder if it looked like
Slim Pickens riding that
Nuclear bomb.

Not:

I bet those cavemen
Named the first domesticated dog
Sparky.
You knew my dad was a

Fire fighter, right.
He named everything
Sparky.
He called my brother and me
Sparky 1 and Sparky 2.
My dad never numbered my sisters.
They were both Sparkettas.
I suppose he thought it was funny.
When I was a kid my friends
and I used to light fires
just so I could see my dad.
He was always working overtime.
My mother slept on the couch
Listening to the
Static saturated frequencies
Of the scanner.

This is what you tell a person who is dying:

Silence
Is like a snowflake
Melting on a window
As if a ghost kisses you
Goodnight and then
You're gone.

Silence between the leaves

after Jürg Frey

The wind

in maples,
pin cherry,
beech and birch

sounds like a ship
bow down
in rough seas,

a heave of green water
washing the leaves,
and then a silence,

curtained,

as if drowning.

About The Author

Michael McInnis lives in Boston and served in the Navy chasing white whales and Soviet submarines. His poetry and short fiction has appeared in *Chiron Review, Cream City Review, Deadly Writers Patrol, Naugatuck Review, Oxford Magazine, Unlikely Stories* and *Yellow Chair Review* to name a few. He was the founder of the Primal Plunge, Boston's only bookstore dedicated to 'zines, underground culture, and small press literature. His previous two books, *Hitchhiking Beatitudes* and *Smokey of the Migraines* were both published by Nixes Mate Books.

CPSIA information can be obtained
at www.ICGtesting.com
Printed in the USA
FSHW011453160919
62060FS